Editor
Mary S. Jones, M.A.

Cover Artist
Delia Rubio

Editor in Chief
Karen J. Goldfluss, M.S. Ed.

Illustrator
Greg Anderson-Clift

Art Production Manager
Kevin Barnes

Imaging
Leonard P. Swierski

Publisher
Mary D. Smith, M.S. Ed.

EARLY LANGUAGE SKILLS

Beginning to Read

GRADES K-1

- Standards-based
- Real Learning
- Really Fun!

Teacher Created Resources

Author

Hunter Calder

Teacher Created Resources, Inc.
6421 Industry Way
Westminster, CA 92683
www.teachercreated.com

ISBN: 978-1-4206-8068-3

© *2008 Teacher Created Resources, Inc.*
Made in U.S.A.

Teacher Created Resources

Table of Contents

Introduction

The delightful illustrations and short, simple exercises in the *Early Language Skills* series will help young learners develop essential language skills with confidence. Each standards-based activity focuses on a specific skill. Clear instructions and examples will guide teachers and parents to help children complete the lessons successfully. Since each page includes a suggestion for extending the learning and reinforcing the skill, the books are ideal for any setting—a classroom, small-group tutoring, or at-home learning.

What's in This Book?

The first half of this book reviews the alphabet and the letter sounds with students. Once students have practiced putting sounds together to make words and writing simple words, they can move on to the second half of the book. Here they will begin reading and understanding simple sentences. Through using the activities in this book, students will:

- learn the letters of the alphabet
- match pictures to the letter they begin with
- match pictures to words
- practice writing simple words from pictures
- read simple sentences and understand their meaning
- develop comprehension skills by reading simple short stories

Work actively with students through each activity so that they understand what they are expected to do on each page. Read the instructions for each activity aloud to the students and model an example. Use the certificates on the next page to reward students for their hard work after they have completed a majority of the activities.

Features of Pages

INSTRUCTIONS — What students need to do for the activity.

EXAMPLE — The first one is done for students so they can see exactly what to do.

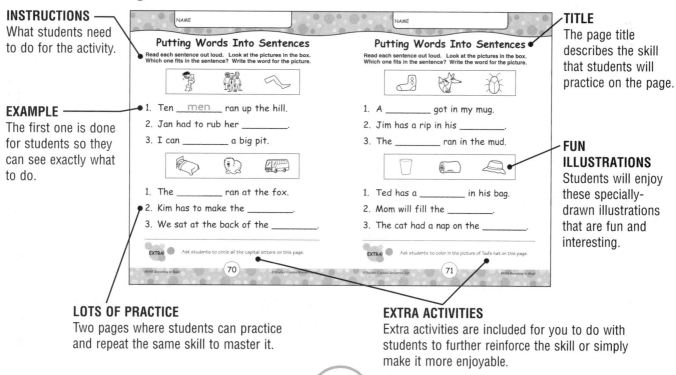

TITLE — The page title describes the skill that students will practice on the page.

FUN ILLUSTRATIONS — Students will enjoy these specially-drawn illustrations that are fun and interesting.

LOTS OF PRACTICE — Two pages where students can practice and repeat the same skill to master it.

EXTRA ACTIVITIES — Extra activities are included for you to do with students to further reinforce the skill or simply make it more enjoyable.

This award goes to

_____

for working
so hard!

Date _____

Congratulations to

_____

for improving your
language skills!

Date _____

Standards and Benchmarks

The activities in this book meet the following standards, which are used with permission from McREL.

Copyright 2006 McREL. Mid-continent Research for Education and Learning.
Address: 2250 S. Parker Road, Suite 500, Aurora, CO 80014
Telephone: 303-377-0990 Website: *www.mcrel.org/standards-benchmarks*

Standard 5.   Uses the general skills and strategies of the reading process

Level I (Grades K–2)

1. Uses mental images based on pictures and print to aid in comprehension of text
3. Uses basic elements of phonetic analysis (e.g., common letter/sound relationships, beginning and ending consonants, vowel sounds, blends, word patterns) to decode unknown words

---

Vowel Sounds

Say each line out loud.

a as in

o as in

e as in

u as in

i as in

 **EXTRA!** It is important that students learn these sounds. Use these pages to practice beginning sounds if they are having difficulty.

6

Consonant Sounds

Say each line out loud.

b as in

g as in

c as in

h as in

d as in

j as in

f as in

 EXTRA! Ask students to tell you what sound each picture ends with.

©*Teacher Created Resources, Inc.*   *#8068 Beginning to Read*

Consonant Sounds

Say each line out loud.

k as in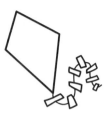

p as in

l as in

q as in

m as in

r as in

n as in

 Ask students to think about what other things would match these letter sounds.

Consonant Sounds

Say each line out loud.

S as in

X as in

t as in

Y as in

V as in

Z as in

W as in

EXTRA! Note: The picture for **x** (ax) represents its ending sound.

9

Learning the Alphabet

Say each line out loud.

a is for

b is for

c is for

d is for

e is for

f is for

g is for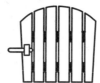

 **EXTRA!** Ask students to color all the pictures that end with the "t" sound.

Learning the Alphabet

Say each line out loud.

h is for

i is for

j is for

k is for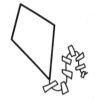

l is for

m is for

 **EXTRA!**   Once the letters are learned, point to each one and have students say its name.

Learning the Alphabet

Say each line out loud.

n is for

o is for

p is for

q is for

r is for

s is for

 **EXTRA!** Ask students to draw a picture that begins with a particular letter.

Learning the Alphabet

Say each line out loud.

t is for

U is for

V is for

W is for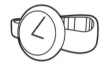

X is for

Y is for

Z is for

 **EXTRA!** Ask students to color all the pictures that end with the "n" sound.

Finding the One that Doesn't Belong to Letters A-D

Put an X on the picture that does not begin with the letter on the left.

a 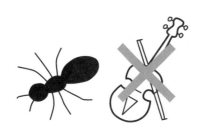   c

b    d

c    a

d    b

EXTRA! Ask students to color in the picture on this page that begins with the letter "s."

Finding the One that Doesn't Belong to Letters E–H

Put an ✗ on the picture that does not begin with the letter on the left.

f		h	
g		e	
h		g	
e		f	

EXTRA! Ask students to color in the picture on this page that begins with the letter "k."

15

Identifying Beginning Letters A-D

What letter does each picture begin with? Circle the correct letter for each picture.

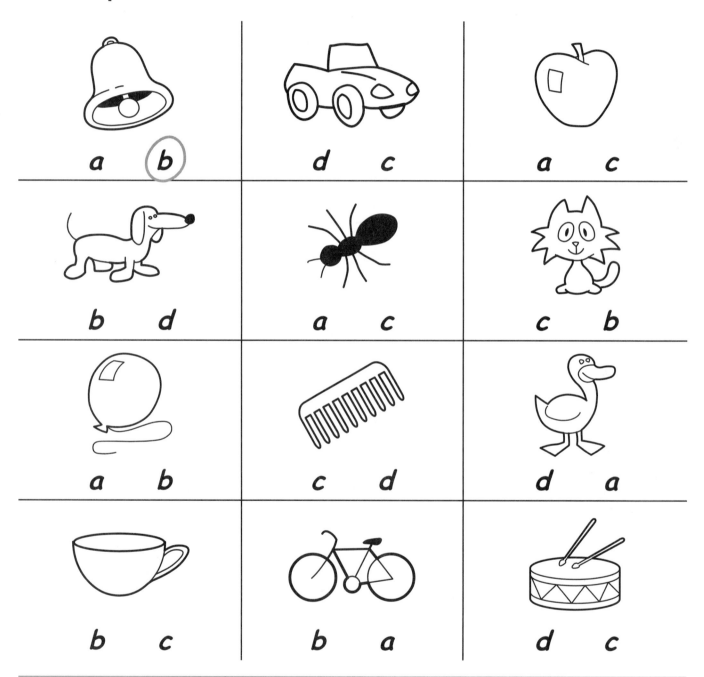

a ⓑ	d c	a c
b d	a c	c b
a b	c d	d a
b c	b a	d c

EXTRA! Ask students to think of something that begins with each of the letters they have not circled on the page.

Identifying Beginning Letters E-H

What letter does each picture begin with? Circle the correct letter for each picture.

h   f   g   f   e   h

e   f   h   g   e   g

h   f   g   e   h   g

g   h   h   e   f   e

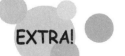 **EXTRA!**   Ask students to color in the pictures on this page that begin with the letter "g."

17

Finding the Letters A-D

Look at the letters in the box at the top of the page.   Then find the letters in the picture and circle them in the correct color.

a	b	c	d
red	blue	green	orange

 **EXTRA!**   *Color in the clown's hair, nose, and feet in red.*

©*Teacher Created Resources, Inc.*

Finding the Letters E-H

Look at the letters in the box at the top of the page. Then find the letters in the picture and circle them in the correct color.

e	f	g	h
blue	yellow	brown	green

 **EXTRA!** Color the snowman's arms brown, his hat black, and his nose orange.

19

Matching Pictures to Letters A-D

Say the name of each picture. Match each picture to the box with the letter that the picture starts with. Then trace the letter in the box.

a   b   c   d

a   c   d   b

EXTRA!  Ask students if they can tell you the letter that each picture ends with.

Matching Pictures to Letters E-H

Say the name of each picture. Match each picture to the box with the letter that the picture starts with. Then trace the letter in the box.

| g | h | e | f |

 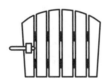 

| f | h | g | e |

 **EXTRA!** Ask students to color all the pictures that end with the letter "t."

©Teacher Created Resources, Inc. #8068 Beginning to Read

Matching Pictures to Words A–D

Match each picture to its name.

box

drum

apple

cake

EXTRA!

Ask students what color starts with the letter "b." What picture on this page starts with "b"? Ask students to color it in a "b" color.

(22)

Matching Pictures to Words E-H

Match each picture to its name.

gate

egg

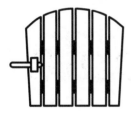

house

fish

EXTRA!

Draw a pattern of letters and ask students to continue the pattern.

23

Finding the Right Word A-D

Say the name of each picture. Then look at the words. Circle the word that matches each picture.

	(ant) art		bell bull
	bell ball		cat cap
	can car		ape ate
	dog dot		deck duck

 **EXTRA!** Ask students to color in the picture that ends with the letter "r."

Finding the Right Word E-H

Say the name of each picture. Then look at the words. Circle the word that matches each picture.

 fish
dish

 peel
eel

 hole
home

 goat
got

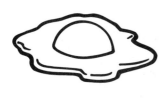 eat
egg

 hind
hand

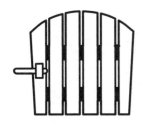 gate
game

 fire
fair

 **EXTRA!** *Ask students to color in the picture that ends with the letter "d."*

Finding the One that Doesn't Belong to Letters I–L

Put an ✗ on the picture that does not begin with the letter on the left.

Ask students to color in the picture on this page that begins with the letter "d."

(26)

Finding the One that Doesn't Belong to Letters M-P

Put an ✗ on the picture that does not begin with the letter on the left.

m		n	
n		o	
o	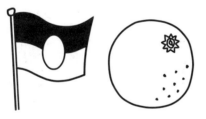	p	
p	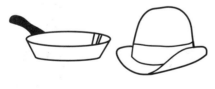	m	

 **EXTRA!** Ask students to color in the picture on this page that begins with the letter "h."

Identifying Beginning Letters I-L

What letter does each picture begin with? Circle the correct letter for each picture.

i *j*	*k* *l*	*j* *l*
j *k*	*l* *i*	*l* *k*
i *j*	*k* *i*	*l* *j*
l *k*	*i* *j*	*k* *j*

 **EXTRA!**

Play a simple game of "I Spy" with students around the classroom by narrowing down the area to search. Can they find a toy that begins with a particular letter? a certain color? something on the table?

28

Identifying Beginning Letters M-P

What letter does each picture begin with? Circle the correct letter for each picture.

m n	o p	n o
m p	o n	p o
n m	n o	p m
n p	o m	o p

 **EXTRA!** Ask students what color starts with the letter "o" (orange). Is there a picture on this page that should be orange? Ask students to color in the picture in orange.

  #8068 Beginning to Read

Finding the Letters I-L

Look at the letters in the box at the top of the page. Then find the letters in the picture and circle them in the correct color.

i	j	k	l
red	blue	green	pink

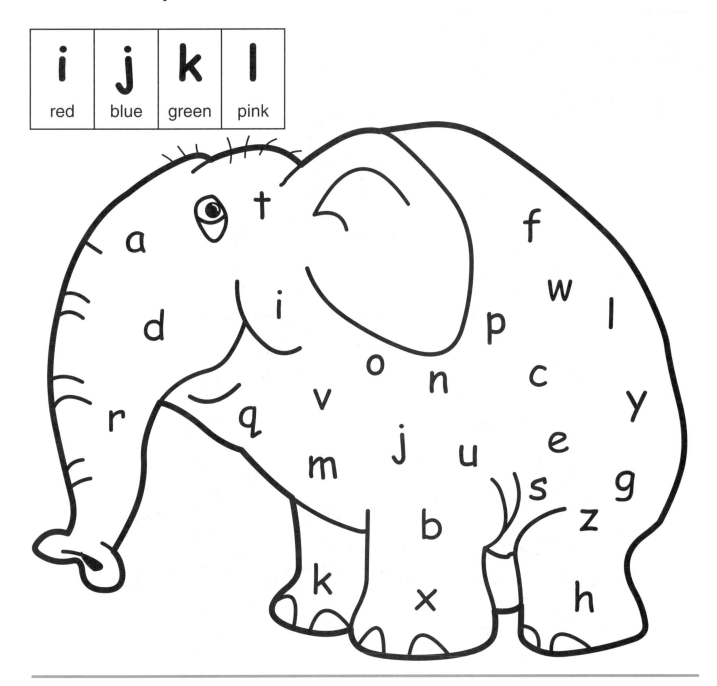

EXTRA! For alphabet practice, write each letter of the alphabet on a separate card. Then ask students to match a group of objects or pictures to the correct card.

30

Finding the Letters M-P

Look at the letters in the box at the top of the page.   Then find the letters in the picture and circle them in the correct color.

m	n	o	p
blue	green	orange	yellow

EXTRA!

Having a magnetic set of alphabet letters on the board is a great way to help students become more familiar with letters.

31

Matching Pictures to Letters I-L

Say the name of each picture. Match each picture to the box with the letter that the picture starts with. Then trace the letter in the box.

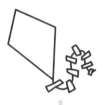  

| l | k | i | j |

| j | l | i | k |

EXTRA!  Ask students to color in the pictures on this page that begin with the letter "j."

Matching Pictures to Letters M-P

Say the name of each picture. Match each picture to the box with the letter that the picture starts with. Then trace the letter in the box.

 m   p   n   o

 m   n   p   o

 **EXTRA!**   Ask students to color in the pictures on this page that begin with the letter "m."

(33)

Matching Pictures to Words I–L

Match each picture to its name.

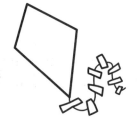

kite

igloo

leaf

jet

EXTRA!

 In one half of the room, try to find as many things as you can that start with the letters on this page. Then move to the other side, or try looking for objects that start with different letters.

34

Matching Pictures to Words M-P

Match each picture to its name.

nurse

moon

penguin

octopus

Ask students what colors start with the letter "p." What picture on this page starts with "p"? Ask students to color it in pink or purple.

Finding the Right Word I–L

Say the name of each picture. Then look at the words. Circle the word that matches each picture.

dice
(ice)

kick
kiss

jet
jem

lion
line

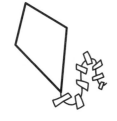
kite
kind

jar
jug

leaf
lean

lion
iron

EXTRA!   Ask students to color in the picture that ends with the letter "f."

36

Finding the Right Word M-P

Say the name of each picture. Then look at the words. Circle the word that matches each picture.

 mood
moon

 neck
deck

 nice
nest

 pool
peel

 ox
fox

 map
mop

 pan
pen

 over
open

EXTRA! Play a basic alphabet game with the letters on this page using simple categories. For example, what things do students eat that begin with m, n, o, p (e.g., marshmallows, nuts, oranges, peas)?

 #8068 Beginning to Read

Finding the One that Doesn't Belong to Letters Q–U

Put an ✗ on the picture that does not begin with the letter on the left.

q			r		
r			t		
s			q		
t			u		
u			s		

Ask students to color in the picture on this page that begins with the letter "m."

Finding the One that Doesn't Belong to Letters V–Z

Put an ✗ on the picture that does not begin with the letter on the left.

EXTRA! Ask students to color in the picture on this page that begins with the letter "e."

#8068 Beginning to Read

Identifying Beginning Letters Q–U

What letter does each picture begin with? Circle the correct letter for each picture.

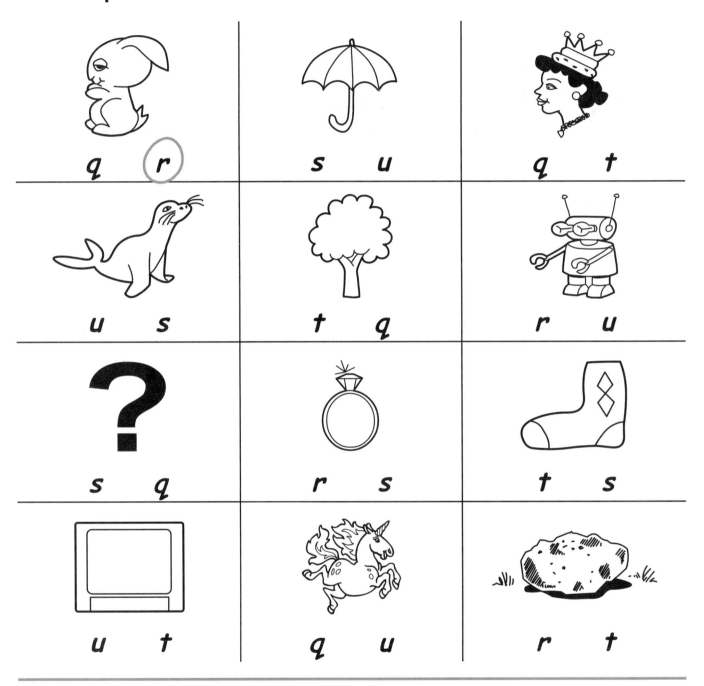

q (r)	s u	q t
u s	t q	r u
s q	r s	t s
u t	q u	r t

EXTRA!

What pictures on this page start with "r"? Ask students to color them in red.

Identifying Beginning Letters V–Z

What letter does each picture begin with? Circle the correct letter for each picture.

    #8068 Beginning to Read

EXTRA!   Ask students to color in the pictures on this page that begin with the letter "v."

Finding the Letters Q-U

Look at the letters in the box at the top of the page. Then find the letters in the picture and circle them in the correct color.

q	r	s	t	u
red	blue	yellow	green	orange

 **EXTRA!** Go for a walk outside to look for signs that have particular letters in them.

Finding the Letters V-Z

Look at the letters in the box at the top of the page.   Then find the letters in the picture and circle them in the correct color.

v	w	x	y	z
orange	green	yellow	blue	pink

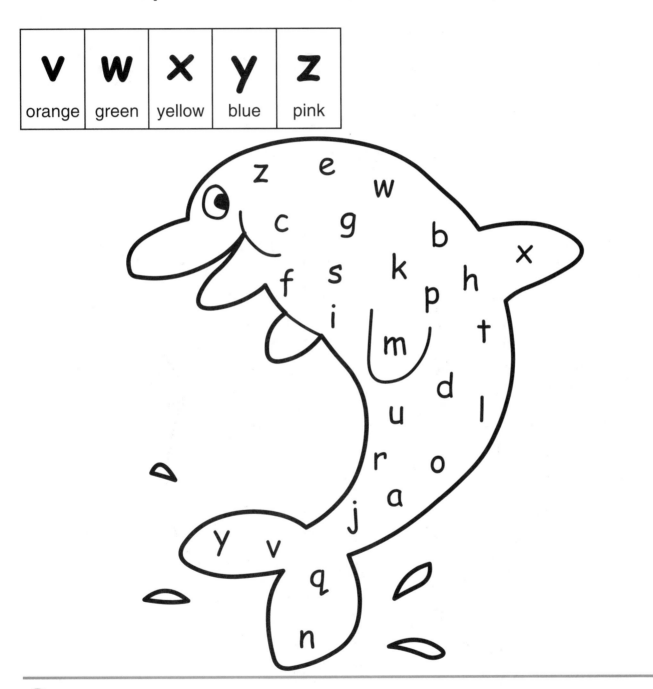

EXTRA!

Play the "alphabet game" with students. Go for a walk and try to find each letter of the alphabet on signs around you.

43

Matching Pictures to Letters Q-U

Say the name of each picture. Match each picture to the box with the letter that the picture starts with. Then trace the letter in the box.

 r   q   s   u

 q   r   s   t

 **EXTRA!** Ask students to color in the pictures on this page that begin with the letter "r."

Matching Pictures to Letters V-Z

Say the name of each picture. Match each picture to the box with the letter that the picture starts with. Then trace the letter in the box.

| v | y | w | z |

| w | y | z | x |

 **EXTRA!** Ask students to color in the pictures on this page that begin with the letter "v."

Matching Pictures to Words Q-U

Match each picture to its name.

ring

unicorn

top

queen

seal

EXTRA! Ask students to put a check next to the picture that begins with the letter "t."

Matching Pictures to Words V-Z

Match each picture to its name.

x-ray

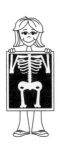

vase

zebra

watch

yawn

 **EXTRA!** Ask students what color starts with the letter "y" (yellow). What picture on this page starts with "y"? Ask students to color it in yellow.

47

Finding the Right Word Q-U

Say the name of each picture. Then look at the words. Circle the word that matches each picture.

queen
quail

thunder
under

rock
rack

tap
top

song
sock

ring
rang

tree
three

sing
sink

EXTRA! Ask students to color in the picture that rhymes with "mop."

(48)

Finding the Right Word V–Z

Say the name of each picture. Then look at the words. Circle the word that matches each picture.

vest
vent

zero
zebra

warm
worm

well
wall

fax
ax

vice
vase

yawn
yarn

zip
zap

 **EXTRA!**   Ask students to color in the picture that rhymes with "nest."

   #8068 Beginning to Read

Reviewing the Alphabet

What letter does each picture begin with? Circle the correct letter for each picture.

a (m) v   w b u   c x d

f e y   f d i   g j i

h s a   z i b   p e c

 **EXTRA!** Ask students to think of something that begins with each of the letters that they have not circled on the page.

Reviewing the Alphabet

What letter does each picture begin with? Circle the correct letter for each picture.

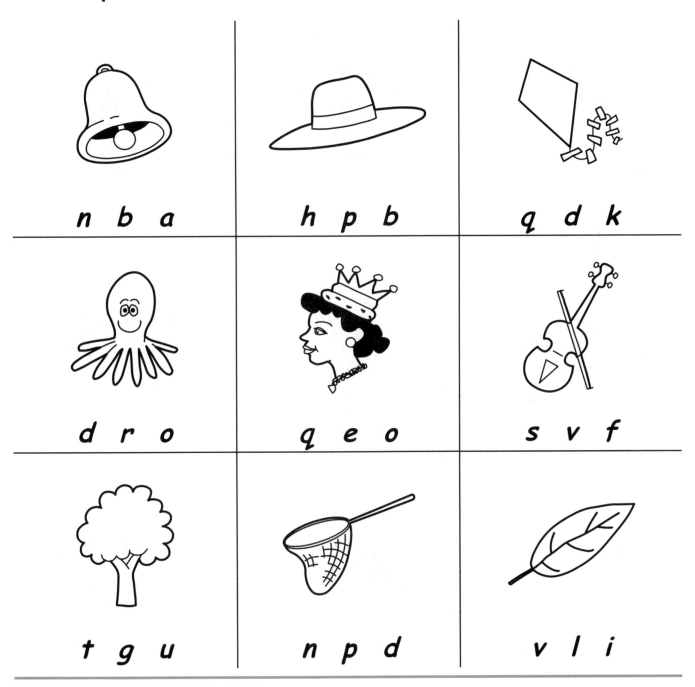

n b a	h p b	q d k
d r o	q e o	s v f
t g u	n p d	v l i

EXTRA!   Ask students to color in the picture on this page that begins with the letter "k."

©*Teacher Created Resources, Inc.*   *#8068 Beginning to Read*

Learning Capital Letters

Match each lowercase letter to its capital.

a   b   c   d   e   f

C   A   E   B   F   D

g   h   i   j   k   l   m

H   K   L   G   J   M   I

EXTRA! Help students understand capital letters by helping them write their name or the name of a family member or friend. Explain how capital letters are used at the beginning of people's names.

Learning Capital Letters

Match each lowercase letter to its capital.

n   o   p   q   r   s

P   N   R   O   S   Q

- -

t   u   v   w   x   y   z

V   Z   T   Y   U   X   W

EXTRA! When students are more familiar with capital letters, cover up the top row of each activity and ask students to say the sounds for the capital letters.

     #8068 Beginning to Read

Writing Words for Pictures

Read each sentence out loud. Then write the word for the picture on the line beside it.

1. Mom has a red  .   sock _____

2. Jen and Mom had a .   _____

3. The sat on the log.   _____

4. Jack got in the  .   _____

5. Dad is in his  .   _____

6. The man has a big  .   _____

EXTRA! You will need to help students understand what a sentence is, and help them sound out the words in each one. Then, before writing the words for the pictures, ask them to write each sound in the word as they say it.

Writing Words for Pictures

Read each sentence out loud. Then write the word for the picture on the line beside it.

1. A big  is in the web. _____

2. Kim has a  . _____

3. The red 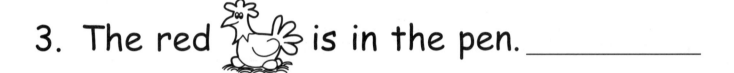 is in the pen. _____

4. Max cut his  . _____

5. The sat on the rock. _____

6. We got hot in the . _____

EXTRA! Ask students a question about each sentence as they complete it. For example, "Who cut his leg?" (Max) or "What does Kim have?" (a doll). This will help their comprehension.

Putting Words Into Sentences

Read each sentence out loud.   Look at the pictures in the box. Which one fits in the sentence?   Write the word for the picture.

1. Jim is ____sick____ in his bed.

2. The red hen fell in the _____.

3. The dog ran at the big _____.

1. We will run up the _____.

2. Rob and Jen ran in the _____.

3. The bag fell in the _____.

EXTRA!

You will need to help students understand what a sentence is, and help them sound out the words in each one. Then, before writing the words for the pictures, ask them to write each sound in the word as they say it.

56

Putting Words Into Sentences

Read each sentence out loud. Look at the pictures in the box. Which one fits in the sentence? Write the word for the picture.

1. Tess can _____ on the bed.

2. Ben will _____ it at us!

3. Dan got the bug in his _____.

1. A _____ is on the well.

2. Tom fell in the _____.

3. The man has a red _____.

 **EXTRA!** It is useful for students to know the difference between capital letters and lower case letters. Show them how the "big" letters are used at the beginning of sentences and for the names of people.

57

Understanding Words

Look at each picture, then read the words below it. If the words tell what the picture is about, put a check in the Yes box. If they do not, put a check in the No box.

a big kid

Yes ☐   No ✓

ten men at the well

Yes ☐   No ☐

a cat on a rug

Yes ☐   No ☐

a rat in a bag

Yes ☐   No ☐

EXTRA!

It is important for this activity that students can read the words "Yes" and "No." Make sure they understand what they need to do for this activity.

Understanding Words

Look at each picture, then read the words below it. If the words tell what the picture is about, put a check in the Yes box. If they do not, put a check in the No box.

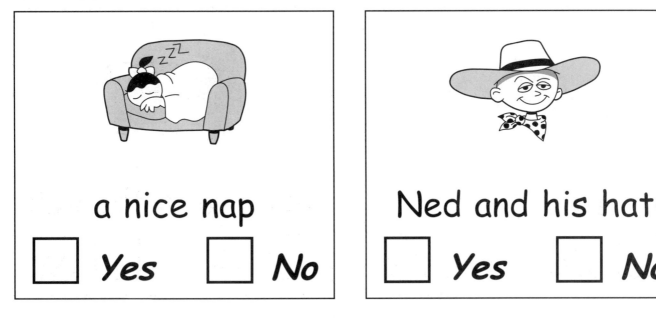

a nice nap

☐ Yes ☐ No

Ned and his hat

☐ Yes ☐ No

six kids on the bus

☐ Yes ☐ No

dig in the mud

☐ Yes ☐ No

EXTRA!

Sing some common nursery rhymes with students, then ask them yes/no questions about what happens in each one. For example, "Did Humpty Dumpty sit on a chair?"

©Teacher Created Resources, Inc.

Choosing the Right Sentence

Look at each picture, then read the sentences underneath it. Which sentence matches the picture? Put a check next to the correct sentence.

He has a big fin. ☐

He has a big pin. ✓

Kim is in her bed. ☐

Kim is in her red. ☐

Jack likes his bat. ☐

Jack likes to tap. ☐

A doll is on a rock. ☐

A doll is in a sock. ☐

EXTRA! Try cutting simple pictures from magazines and helping students write simple sentences to describe them. The sentences would need to be very simple, such as "A man has a hat" or "A dog on a rug."

Choosing the Right Sentence

Look at each picture, then read the sentences underneath it. Which sentence matches the picture? Put a check next to the correct sentence.

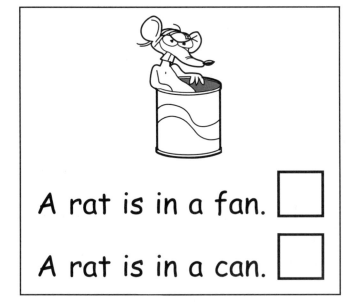

A rat is in a fan. ☐

A rat is in a can. ☐

A pup sits on a rug. ☐

A pup sits in a mug. ☐

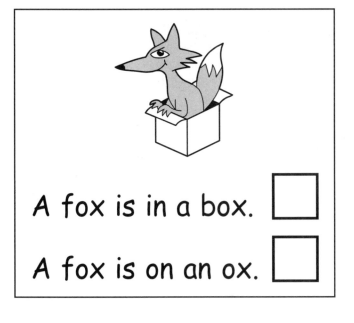

A fox is in a box. ☐

A fox is on an ox. ☐

A tap is on Ben. ☐

A cap is on Ben. ☐

EXTRA!

You could do this activity using simple pictures from magazines or photos. Write two simple sentences and ask students to check the correct one.

Choosing the Right Word

Read each sentence out loud. Which word doesn't belong? Circle the correct word in the sentence.

1. A **duck** / **luck** is on the dock.

2. Jan has a **bed** / **red** pen.

3. The man **hat** / **sat** in the van.

4. Mom will **cut** / **hut** the bun.

5. Will has a **big** / **dig** hat.

6. Dad will **rock** / **lock** the box.

EXTRA! Ask students to find all the words on this page that begin with the "r" sound. How many are there? Ask them to underline each one.

Choosing the Right Word

Read each sentence out loud. Which word doesn't belong?
Circle the correct word in the sentence.

1. Ben has to *wet / get* a job.

2. Jan has to sell the big *dog / fog*.

3. Pam *fell / bell* off her bed.

4. Mom has a *rap / cap* in her bag.

5. Bess sat in the *hot / pot* tub.

6. Dad will *rub / cub* my back.

EXTRA! Ask students to find all the words on this page that begin with the "b" sound. How many are there? Ask them to underline each one. Can they recognize the capital "B" in "Bess" and "Ben"?

Copying Words Into Sentences

Read each sentence out loud, then read the words in the box. Which one fits in the sentence? Write in the missing word.

back	**doll**	**sat**

1. Six men ___sat___ on the log.

2. Pam has a _____ in a box.

3. Ross has a pack on his _____.

rub	**dog**	**ran**

1. The _____ had a nap in the sun.

2. Mom will _____ my leg.

3. The cat _____ at the big rat.

EXTRA! Students could draw a simple picture to illustrate one of the correct sentences on the page. For example, they might draw a doll in a box, or a dog asleep in the sun.

64

Copying Words Into Sentences

Read each sentence out loud, then read the words in the box. Which one fits in the sentence? Write in the missing word.

rug	got	fell

1. Tim got mud on the _____.

2. My hat _____ off the dock.

3. Ben and his dad _____ in the van.

mug	red	jog

1. Jan had a _____ up the hill.

2. Nan will fill my _____.

3. The big _____ jug is in the box.

EXTRA! What color is the jug in the last sentence on this page? Ask students to draw a picture of it.

Reading a Story

Read the story, then read the sentences underneath it. Write in the missing words from the story.

It was hot in the sun! The dog was hot. The hen was fat and hot. The dog sat on a log. The hen sat by a rock. A cat got on the rock. The dog ran at the cat. The hen got in the log. The hen was not hot in the log.

1. The dog sat on a ____log____.

2. The hen sat by a _____.

3. The _____ ran at the cat.

4. The _____ was not hot in the log.

 Ask students questions to help their comprehension of the story. Why was it hot? Who got in the log?

©Teacher Created Resources, Inc.

Reading a Story

Choose a word from the box to fill each space in the story.

not	hen	hot	sat	rock

It was _____ in the sun! The dog was

hot. The hen was fat and hot. The dog

_____ on a log. The hen sat by a

_____. A cat got on the rock. The dog

ran at the cat. The _____ got in the

log. The hen was _____ hot in the log.

 **EXTRA!** Help students understand the story by acting out parts of it together. Can they pretend to be a dog chasing a cat?

©Teacher Created Resources, Inc. #8068 Beginning to Read

Writing Words for Pictures

Read each sentence out loud. Then write the word for the picture on the line beside it.

1. The cat is in the .   __bag__

2. Jill got a 🐞 in the net.   _____

3. Ross can hop off the 🪵 .   _____

4. The kid has a rip in his 👕 . _____

5. We will 👊 the can.   _____

6. The 📦 fell in the mud.   _____

EXTRA! Ask students a question about each sentence as they complete it. For example, "What is in Jill's net?" (bug) or "Who can hop off the log?" (Ross).

#8068 *Beginning to Read*

Writing Words for Pictures

Read each sentence out loud. Then write the word for the picture on the line beside it.

1. The 🐕 sat on the rug. _____

2. Mom has an 🍳 in the pan. _____

3. Jess has a red 🎩. _____

4. The 🧢 fell off the bed. _____

5. We can 🧍 in the pit. _____

6. A bug sat on the 🪨. _____

EXTRA! Ask students to color in the pictures after they complete the page.

Putting Words Into Sentences

Read each sentence out loud.   Look at the pictures in the box.
Which one fits in the sentence? Write the word for the picture.

1. Ten ____men____ ran up the hill.

2. Jan had to rub her _____.

3. I can _____ a big pit.

1. The _____ ran at the fox.

2. Kim has to make the _____.

3. We sat at the back of the _____.

EXTRA!   Ask students to circle all the capital letters on this page.

70

Putting Words Into Sentences

**Read each sentence out loud. Look at the pictures in the box.
Which one fits in the sentence? Write the word for the picture.**

1. A _____ got in my mug.

2. Jim has a rip in his _____.

3. The _____ ran in the mud.

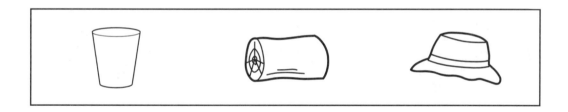

1. Ted has a _____ in his bag.

2. Mom will fill the _____.

3. The cat had a nap on the _____.

 **EXTRA!** Ask students to color in the picture of Ted's hat on this page.

Understanding Words

Look at each picture, then read the words below it. If the words tell what the picture is about, put a check in the Yes box. If they do not, put a check in the No box.

on top of a hill

☑ Yes ☐ No

a gull on the bed

☐ Yes ☐ No

a cut on my leg

☐ Yes ☐ No

fun in the tub

☐ Yes ☐ No

 **EXTRA!** Try your own version of this activity using photographs of students. Write a sentence about each one, and ask students to read it and say if it is correct or not.

©Teacher Created Resources, Inc.

Understanding Words

Look at each picture, then read the words below it. If the words tell what the picture is about, put a check in the Yes box. If they do not, put a check in the No box.

a dog in the sun

☐ Yes ☐ No

fun with a top

☐ Yes ☐ No

Jill on the rock

☐ Yes ☐ No

a mug and a cup

☐ Yes ☐ No

 **EXTRA!** There are two words on this page that rhyme with "run." Ask students to circle them.

Choosing the Right Sentence

Look at each picture, then read the sentences underneath it. Which sentence matches the picture? Put a check next to the correct sentence.

I have a pet bug. ✓

I have a pet dog. ☐

The dog has a net. ☐

The dog is wet. ☐

She sees the big sun. ☐

She cuts the big bun. ☐

Jen is six. ☐

Jen is mix. ☐

 **EXTRA!** Write "Yes" and "No" on different cards. Then ask students yes/no questions and ask them to hold up the correct card.

Choosing the Right Sentence

Look at each picture, then read the sentences underneath it. Which sentence matches the picture? Put a check next to the correct sentence.

She runs in the sun. ☐

She sings in the sun. ☐

We had a big mug. ☐

We had a big hug. ☐

Sam has a jog. ☐

Sam has a frog. ☐

A duck is in the tub. ☐

A duck is in the rub. ☐

EXTRA!

Ask students to find the words on this page that end with the letter "g" and circle them.

75

Choosing the Right Word

**Read each sentence out loud. Which word doesn't belong?
Circle the correct word in the sentence.**

1. Ten of us (got) / *pot* on the bus.

2. Mom will mop *up* / *cup* the mess.

3. The red fox *pan* / *ran* at the hen.

4. Jim will *run* / *fun* to his mom.

5. Jen is on *top* / *hop* of the rock.

6. Dan will fill his *dug* / *mug*.

EXTRA! Ask students to find all the words on this page which begin with the letter "f." How many are there? Ask them to underline each one.

Choosing the Right Word

Read each sentence out loud. Which word doesn't belong?
Circle the correct word in the sentence.

1. Tim has a **cut / but** on his leg.

2. The pup had a **tap / nap** on the rug.

3. The **tug / jug** is in the box.

4. Mom **fill / will** hug Kim and Jen.

5. The **dig / wig** is on my Dad.

6. The man will fill the **bag / rag**.

EXTRA! Ask students to find all the words on this page which begin with the letter "h." How many are there? Ask them to underline each one.

©*Teacher Created Resources, Inc.*

Copying Words Into Sentences

Read each sentence out loud, then read the words in the box. Which one fits in the sentence? Write in the missing word.

box	sat	run

1. Can you ___run___ to the well.

2. Jack has a lock on the _____.

3. We _____ in the back of the bus.

bib	duck	fat

1. My pet _____ is on the rock.

2. Kim has a mess on her _____.

3. Tom can pat the _____ cat.

 **EXTRA!** Ask students to draw a simple picture to illustrate one of the correct sentences on the page.

Copying Words Into Sentences

**Read each sentence out loud, then read the words in the box.
Which one fits in the sentence? Write in the missing word.**

sick	**sun**	**sit**

1. The dog is in the _____.

2. Jill will _____ on the log.

3. Rob is _____ in his bed.

yell	**hop**	**dog**

1. Dad had to _____ at the bad cat.

2. My _____ can lick his leg.

3. Ten men will _____ off the rock.

EXTRA!   Where is the dog sitting in the first sentence of this page?
Ask students to draw a picture of it.

Reading a Story

Read the story, then read the sentences underneath it. Write in the missing words from the story.

Jeff and Jill dug in the mud. Dig, dig, dig.
Jeff dug and dug. His cap fell in the mud.
Jill dug and dug. Her red hat fell in the mud.
The cap was a mess. The red hat was a mess.
"Yuck!" said Jeff and Jill. "We will run and see
Mom. She will fix the mess!"

1. Jeff and Jill dug in the __mud__.

2. His cap _____ in the mud.

3. The red _____ was a mess.

Ask students questions to help their comprehension of the story. Who was digging in the mud? What happened to the red hat?

Reading a Story

Choose a word from the box to fill each space in the story.

run	dug	fix	cap	red	mess

Jeff and Jill _____ in the mud.

Dig, dig, dig. Jeff dug and dug. His

_____ fell in the mud. Jill dug and

dug. Her _____ hat fell in the mud.

The cap was a mess. The red hat was

a _____. "Yuck!" said Jeff and Jill.

"We will _____ and see Mom. She will

_____ the mess!"

EXTRA! Help students understand the story by acting out parts of it together. Can students pretend to be digging in the mud?

 #8068 Beginning to Read

Writing Words for Pictures

Read each sentence out loud. Then write the word for the picture on the line beside it.

1. Jan will off the dock. _hop_

2. I had to up the mess. _____

3. Tim sat at the . _____

4. We ran to get on the . _____

5. The big  is in a box. _____

6. A is on my mug. _____

 **EXTRA!** Ask students a question about each sentence as they complete it. For example, "Where did Tim sit?" (at the well) or "Who will hop off the dock?" (Jan).

#8068 Beginning to Read

Writing Words for Pictures

Read each sentence out loud. Then write the word for the picture on the line beside it.

1. Pam had fun in the  . _____

2. Mom had a ⁄ on the bib. _____

3. The 🦢 sat on top of the rock. _____

4. Dad had to rub my 🦒 . _____

5. Ned will 🔒 up the van. _____

6. Pat has a red  . _____

 **EXTRA!**   Ask students to color in the pictures after they complete the page.

©*Teacher Created Resources, Inc.*   *#8068 Beginning to Read*

Putting Words Into Sentences

**Read each sentence out loud.   Look at the pictures in the box.
Which one fits in the sentence?   Write the word for the picture.**

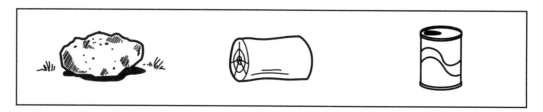

1. The ___log___ can roll off the hill.

2. We can hop off the big _____.

3. Jess has a big tin _____.

1. I had a _____ in my bib.

2. Can you _____ the big can?

3. Jack has a red _____.

 **EXTRA!**   Rewrite each word students write on separate cards. Then ask
them to match up the cards with the words they have written.

84

Putting Words Into Sentences

Read each sentence out loud. Look at the pictures in the box. Which one fits in the sentence? Write the word for the picture.

1. My _____ is in the box.

2. The cat ran at the _____.

3. Nell has a _____ and a hen.

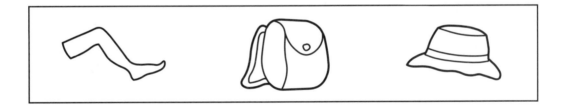

1. Tom has a _____ in his bag.

2. The pup had a nip at my _____.

3. Mom has a _____ in the van.

EXTRA!

Write the words *box, ran, hen, Tom, pup,* and *van* onto separate cards, then shuffle them around. Ask students to find each word on the page and circle it as they go.

Understanding Words

Look at each picture, then read the words below it. If the words tell what the picture is about, put a check in the Yes box. If they do not, put a check in the No box.

on top of the rock

☐ Yes   ✔ No

a hen in my sock

☐ Yes   ☐ No

a mess to mop

☐ Yes   ☐ No

a back rub

☐ Yes   ☐ No

 **EXTRA!**   Write down the words *hen*, *mop*, *doll*, and *wig* on a sheet of paper. Then ask students to find these objects on this double page.

86

Understanding Words

Look at each picture, then read the words below it. If the words tell what the picture is about, put a check in the Yes box. If they do not, put a check in the No box.

a big hat

☐ Yes   ☐ No

cut the bun

☐ Yes   ☐ No

a doll to hug

☐ Yes   ☐ No

a wig for Mom

☐ Yes   ☐ No

EXTRA!

Write "Yes" and "No" on different cards. Then take students outside and ask them yes/no questions about their environment, while they hold up the correct cards.

87

Choosing the Right Sentence

Look at each picture, then read the sentences underneath it. Which sentence matches the picture? Put a check next to the correct sentence.

He cut up the fog. ☐

He cut up the log. ✓

She runs in the mud. ☐

She sits in the mud. ☐

A bug on the jug. ☐

A bug on the rug. ☐

A bat sits on Mom. ☐

A cat sits on Mom. ☐

EXTRA! Ask students to find the words on this page that rhyme with "dog" and circle them. What else rhymes with "dog"?

Choosing the Right Sentence

Look at each picture, then read the sentences underneath it. Which sentence matches the picture? Put a check next to the correct sentence.

My dog is hot. ☐

My dog is not hot. ☐

Mix the tap. ☐

Fix the tap. ☐

An egg is in the pan. ☐

An egg is on the man. ☐

Mop up the mess. ☐

Hop on the mess. ☐

EXTRA!

Write down the words *log, dog, jug,* and *tap* on a sheet of paper. Then ask students to find these objects on pages 88–89.

©*Teacher Created Resources, Inc.*   *#8068 Beginning to Read*

Choosing the Right Word

Read each sentence out loud. Which word doesn't belong?
Circle the correct word in the sentence.

1. Nan has a red **sat** / **hat**.

2. Pop sat on top of the **log** / **fog**.

3. The big **rug** / **bug** is in the web.

4. Ten **pen** / **men** met at the well.

5. Pam got in the **van** / **ran**.

6. Max has a **tin** / **pin** in his bib.

EXTRA! Help students find the right word by reading the sentence together. This will help them recognize the difference between the two similar words.

Choosing the Right Word

Read each sentence out loud. Which word doesn't belong?
Circle the correct word in the sentence.

1. Dan will *fix / six* the tap.

2. Tess got a doll in a *fox / box*.

3. The *bat / sat* is in the bag.

4. Can mom cut up the *run / bun*?

5. Pam is sick in *bed / fed*.

6. The man *fill / will* lock his van.

EXTRA!

Ask students to find all the words on this page that begin with the "s" sound. How many are there? Ask them to underline each one.

©*Teacher Created Resources, Inc.* #*8068 Beginning to Read*

Copying Words Into Sentences

Read each sentence out loud, then read the words in the box. Which one fits in the sentence? Write in the missing word.

log	pan	rub

1. The big dog is on the ___log___.

2. Dad had to _____ his neck.

3. An egg is in the _____.

hen	got	fun

1. Ann had _____ in the big tub.

2. The pup _____ on top of my bed.

3. The fox ran after the _____.

EXTRA! Ask students to draw a simple picture to illustrate one of the correct sentences on the page. For example, they might draw a puppy on a bed, or an egg cooking.

©Teacher Created Resources, Inc.

Copying Words Into Sentences

Read each sentence out loud, then read the words in the box. Which one fits in the sentence? Write in the missing word.

hat	**pack**	**big**

1. Ben has to _____ up his bag.

2. Dad cut the _____ bun.

3. Nell has a red _____.

dug	**rip**	**mat**

1. Did the rat get off the _____?

2. We _____ in the mud.

3. Tess has a _____ in her sock.

EXTRA!   *What kind of a hat does Nell have on this page? Ask students to draw a picture of it.*

Reading a Story

Read the story, then read the sentences underneath it. Write in the missing words from the story.

The red hen had an egg — a big, big egg. Tess and Tom said, "We will get the egg." The red hen said, "No, no, no!" "You will not get my egg! I will peck you on the leg. Peck, peck, peck!" The bad fox ran in the pen to get the hen. A big dog ran at the fox. Tess and Tom got the egg. Tess and Tom said to the red hen, "We got the egg and you did not peck us!" The hen got mad!

1. The red hen had an ____egg____.

2. "You will not _____ my egg!"

3. The bad _____ ran in the pen.

4. A big _____ ran at the fox.

___

EXTRA! Ask students questions to help their comprehension of the story. What color was the hen? Who got the egg?

Reading a Story

Choose a word from the box to fill each space in the story.

hen	Tess	egg	mad	pen

The red hen had an _____ — a big, big egg. Tess and Tom said, "We will get the egg." The red _____ said, "No, no, no! You will not get my egg! I will peck you on the leg. Peck, peck, peck!" The bad fox ran in the _____ to get the hen. A big dog ran at the fox. _____ and Tom got the egg. Tess and Tom said to the red hen, "We got the egg and you did not peck us!" The hen got _____ !

EXTRA! Help students understand the story by acting out parts of it. Can they pretend to be the hen pecking at Tess and Tom?

#8068 Beginning to Read

Reading a Story

Read the story, then look at the two words under each line. For each line, choose the word that best fits into the story. Write the word on the line.

Ben has to _____ a job. He likes
(net, get)

to work with _____. He likes to
(dogs, fogs)

_____ for _____. He will work
(run, bun)   (sun, fun)

as a dog walker. That is a good _____
(sob, job)

for Ben. The dogs _____ and eat.
(sit, pit)

The dogs run and _____. Ben likes his
(play, tray)

_____ job.
(few, new)

EXTRA! Practice this same activity by taking a familiar children's story and leaving out some of the words. Ask students to fill in the blanks with words that make sense.